40 Weeks Journey
Belongs to:

Estimated date of delivery

_____ / _____ / _____

Add Baby Ultrasound Photo Here

Important Things to Note...

Hospital Name :
_____

Hospital Address :
_____

Gynae Name :
_____

Gynae Contact Number :
_____

Time you are born :
_____

Medical History, if any :
_____

Preference of delivery type :
_____

_____

_____

_____

_____

_____

To add on as necessary

Congratulation on your Pregnancy and let's get start your 40 weeks Journey now!

Weekly Weight Tracker for Wife

Week	Weight (KG)	Week	Weight (KG)
1		21	
2		22	
3		23	
4		24	
5		25	
6		26	
7		27	
8		28	
9		29	
10		30	
11		31	
12		32	
13		33	
14		34	
15		35	
16		36	
17		37	
18		38	
19		39	
20		40	

Checklist

Have you prepared for the new arrival ?

Prenatal Appointment

- ☐ Have you book?
- ☐
- ☐
- ☐
- ☐

For the Mommy

- ☐ Mommy's Comfy wear till 5mths
- ☐ Mommy's Comfy wear till birth
- ☐ Breast Pump
- ☐
- ☐
- ☐
- ☐
- ☐
- ☐
- ☐
- ☐
- ☐

Childbirth Classes

- ☐ Have you book?
- ☐
- ☐
- ☐
- ☐

For the Baby

- ☐ Baby's Room
- ☐ Baby's Comfy clothing
- ☐ Baby's Cot
- ☐ Baby's Wash
- ☐
- ☐
- ☐
- ☐
- ☐
- ☐
- ☐

Preparing for Delivery

- ☐ Hospital Bag
- ☐
- ☐
- ☐
- ☐

Others

- ☐
- ☐
- ☐
- ☐
- ☐

Mommy and Baby Health Check

1ST CHECK UP _____

Important notes:

_____

_____

Weight:

_____

_____

Others:

_____

_____

PREPARATION

_____

_____

_____

_____

_____

Mommy and Baby Health Check

2ND CHECK UP _____

Important notes:
_____
_____

Weight:
_____

Others:
_____
_____

PREPARATION

_____
_____
_____
_____
_____

Mommy and Baby Health Check

3RD CHECK UP _____

Important notes:

_____

_____

Weight:

_____

_____

Others:

_____

_____

BABY INFORMATION

Length :

_____

_____

Weight :

_____

_____

Others :

_____

_____

Mommy and Baby Health Check

4TH CHECK UP _____

Important notes:
_____
_____

Weight:
_____

Others:
_____
_____

BABY INFORMATION

Length :
_____

Weight :
_____

Others :
_____
_____

Mommy and Baby Health Check

5TH CHECK UP _____

Important notes:
_____
_____

Weight:
_____
_____

Others:
_____
_____

BABY INFORMATION

Length :
_____

Weight :
_____

Others :
_____
_____

Mommy and Baby Health Check

6TH CHECK UP _____

Important notes:
_____
_____

Weight:
_____

Others:
_____
_____

BABY INFORMATION

Length :
_____

Weight :
_____

Others :
_____
_____

Mommy and Baby Health Check

7TH CHECK UP _____

Important notes:
_____
_____

Weight:
_____
_____

Others:
_____
_____

BABY INFORMATION

Length :
_____

Weight :
_____

Others :
_____
_____

Mommy and Baby Health Check

8TH CHECK UP _____

Important notes:
_____
_____

Weight:
_____

Others:
_____
_____

BABY INFORMATION

Length :
_____

Weight :
_____

Others :
_____
_____

Mommy and Baby Health Check

9TH CHECK UP _____

Important notes:
_____
_____

Weight:
_____
_____

Others:
_____
_____

BABY INFORMATION

Length :
_____

Weight :
_____

Others :
_____

Mommy and Baby Health Check

10TH CHECK UP _____

Important notes:
_____
_____

Weight:
_____
_____

Others:
_____
_____

BABY INFORMATION

Length :
_____
_____

Weight :
_____
_____

Others :
_____
_____

Mommy and Baby Health Check

11TH CHECK UP _____

Important notes:
_____
_____

Weight:
_____

Others:
_____
_____

BABY INFORMATION

Length :
_____

Weight :
_____

Others :
_____
_____

Mommy and Baby Health Check

12TH CHECK UP _____

Important notes:
_____
_____

Weight:
_____
_____

Others:
_____
_____

BABY INFORMATION

Length :
_____
_____

Weight :
_____
_____

Others :
_____
_____

Mommy and Baby Health Check

13TH CHECK UP _____

Important notes:
_____
_____

Weight:
_____
_____

Others:
_____
_____

BABY INFORMATION

Length :
_____

Weight :
_____

Others :
_____
_____

Mommy and Baby Health Check

LAST CHECK UP _____

Important notes:
_____
_____

Weight:
_____
_____

Others:
_____
_____

BABY INFORMATION

Length :
_____

Weight :
_____

Others :
_____

Mommy and Bump Photo

WEEK 1 _____

WEEK 2 _____

Mommy and Bump Photo

WEEK 3 _____

WEEK 4 _____

Mommy and Bump Photo

WEEK 5 _____

WEEK 6 _____

Mommy and Bump Photo

WEEK 7 _____

WEEK 8 _____

Mommy and Bump Photo

WEEK 9 _____

WEEK 10 _____

Mommy and Bump Photo

WEEK 11 _____

WEEK 12 _____

Mommy and Bump Photo

WEEK 13 _____

WEEK 14 _____

Mommy and Bump Photo

WEEK 15 _____

WEEK 16 _____

Mommy and Bump Photo

WEEK 17 _____

WEEK 18 _____

Mommy and Bump Photo

WEEK 19 _____

WEEK 20 _____

Mommy and Bump Photo

WEEK 21 _____

WEEK 22 _____

Mommy and Bump Photo

WEEK 23 _____

WEEK 24 _____

Mommy and Bump Photo

WEEK 25 _____

WEEK 26 _____

Mommy and Bump Photo

WEEK 27 _____

WEEK 28 _____

Mommy and Bump Photo

WEEK 29 _____

WEEK 30 _____

Mommy and Bump Photo

WEEK 31 _____

WEEK 32 _____

Mommy and Bump Photo

WEEK 33 _____

WEEK 34 _____

Mommy and Bump Photo

WEEK 35 _____

WEEK 36 _____

Mommy and Bump Photo

WEEK 37 _____

WEEK 38 _____

Mommy and Bump Photo

WEEK 39 _____

WEEK 40 _____

So Excited – Am I Pink or Blue?

DATE _____

Add Baby Ultrasound Photo Here

The First Trimester (Week 1 to 12)

> Daddy & Mommy to Note:
> Though pregnancy is a happy news but it isn't all sunshine throughout. Mommy will experience some discomfort as the little one is growing each day inside.
> Some wife may experience morning sickness, hence avoid foods that may cause nausea.
> Remember to go for checkup on time.
>
> May practice prenatal yoga with poses that will help to ease discomfort, relieve stress and tired feet.
> Please seek professional advice from instructor who teaches prenatal yoga

Some yoga poses

Utthita Trikonasana
-Extended Triangle Pose

Virabhadrasana I
-Warrior I Pose

Vrksasana - Tree Pose

Baddha Konasana
- Bound Angle Pose

The First Trimester (Week 1)

Weekly Plan Starting _____

Day 1
- ☐ _____
- ☐ _____
- ☐ _____
- ☐ _____
- ☐ _____

Day 2
- ☐ _____
- ☐ _____
- ☐ _____
- ☐ _____
- ☐ _____

Day 3
- ☐ _____
- ☐ _____
- ☐ _____
- ☐ _____
- ☐ _____

Day 4
- ☐ _____
- ☐ _____
- ☐ _____
- ☐ _____
- ☐ _____

Day 5
- ☐ _____
- ☐ _____
- ☐ _____
- ☐ _____
- ☐ _____

Day 6
- ☐ _____
- ☐ _____
- ☐ _____
- ☐ _____
- ☐ _____

Day 7
- ☐ _____
- ☐ _____
- ☐ _____
- ☐ _____
- ☐ _____

Notes
- ☐ _____
- ☐ _____
- ☐ _____
- ☐ _____
- ☐ _____

The First Trimester (Week 2)

Weekly Plan Starting _____

Day 1
- ☐ _____
- ☐ _____
- ☐ _____
- ☐ _____
- ☐ _____

Day 2
- ☐ _____
- ☐ _____
- ☐ _____
- ☐ _____
- ☐ _____

Day 3
- ☐ _____
- ☐ _____
- ☐ _____
- ☐ _____
- ☐ _____

Day 4
- ☐ _____
- ☐ _____
- ☐ _____
- ☐ _____
- ☐ _____

Day 5
- ☐ _____
- ☐ _____
- ☐ _____
- ☐ _____
- ☐ _____

Day 6
- ☐ _____
- ☐ _____
- ☐ _____
- ☐ _____
- ☐ _____

Day 7
- ☐ _____
- ☐ _____
- ☐ _____
- ☐ _____
- ☐ _____

Notes
- ☐ _____
- ☐ _____
- ☐ _____
- ☐ _____
- ☐ _____

The First Trimester (Week 3)

Weekly Plan Starting _____

Day 1
- ☐ _____
- ☐ _____
- ☐ _____
- ☐ _____
- ☐ _____

Day 2
- ☐ _____
- ☐ _____
- ☐ _____
- ☐ _____
- ☐ _____

Day 3
- ☐ _____
- ☐ _____
- ☐ _____
- ☐ _____
- ☐ _____

Day 4
- ☐ _____
- ☐ _____
- ☐ _____
- ☐ _____
- ☐ _____

Day 5
- ☐ _____
- ☐ _____
- ☐ _____
- ☐ _____
- ☐ _____

Day 6
- ☐ _____
- ☐ _____
- ☐ _____
- ☐ _____
- ☐ _____

Day 7
- ☐ _____
- ☐ _____
- ☐ _____
- ☐ _____
- ☐ _____

Notes
- ☐ _____
- ☐ _____
- ☐ _____
- ☐ _____
- ☐ _____

The First Trimester (Week 4)

Weekly Plan Starting _____

Day 1
- ☐ _____
- ☐ _____
- ☐ _____
- ☐ _____
- ☐ _____

Day 2
- ☐ _____
- ☐ _____
- ☐ _____
- ☐ _____
- ☐ _____

Day 3
- ☐ _____
- ☐ _____
- ☐ _____
- ☐ _____
- ☐ _____

Day 4
- ☐ _____
- ☐ _____
- ☐ _____
- ☐ _____
- ☐ _____

Day 5
- ☐ _____
- ☐ _____
- ☐ _____
- ☐ _____
- ☐ _____

Day 6
- ☐ _____
- ☐ _____
- ☐ _____
- ☐ _____
- ☐ _____

Day 7
- ☐ _____
- ☐ _____
- ☐ _____
- ☐ _____
- ☐ _____

Notes
- ☐ _____
- ☐ _____
- ☐ _____
- ☐ _____
- ☐ _____

The First Trimester (Week 5)

Weekly Plan Starting _____

Day 1
- [ ] _____
- [ ] _____
- [ ] _____
- [ ] _____
- [ ] _____

Day 2
- [ ] _____
- [ ] _____
- [ ] _____
- [ ] _____
- [ ] _____

Day 3
- [ ] _____
- [ ] _____
- [ ] _____
- [ ] _____
- [ ] _____

Day 4
- [ ] _____
- [ ] _____
- [ ] _____
- [ ] _____
- [ ] _____

Day 5
- [ ] _____
- [ ] _____
- [ ] _____
- [ ] _____
- [ ] _____

Day 6
- [ ] _____
- [ ] _____
- [ ] _____
- [ ] _____
- [ ] _____

Day 7
- [ ] _____
- [ ] _____
- [ ] _____
- [ ] _____
- [ ] _____

Notes
- [ ] _____
- [ ] _____
- [ ] _____
- [ ] _____
- [ ] _____

The First Trimester (Week 6)

Weekly Plan Starting _____

Day 1
- ☐ _____
- ☐ _____
- ☐ _____
- ☐ _____
- ☐ _____

Day 2
- ☐ _____
- ☐ _____
- ☐ _____
- ☐ _____
- ☐ _____

Day 3
- ☐ _____
- ☐ _____
- ☐ _____
- ☐ _____
- ☐ _____

Day 4
- ☐ _____
- ☐ _____
- ☐ _____
- ☐ _____
- ☐ _____

Day 5
- ☐ _____
- ☐ _____
- ☐ _____
- ☐ _____
- ☐ _____

Day 6
- ☐ _____
- ☐ _____
- ☐ _____
- ☐ _____
- ☐ _____

Day 7
- ☐ _____
- ☐ _____
- ☐ _____
- ☐ _____
- ☐ _____

Notes
- ☐ _____
- ☐ _____
- ☐ _____
- ☐ _____
- ☐ _____

The First Trimester (Week 7)

Weekly Plan Starting _____

Day 1
- [ ] _____
- [ ] _____
- [ ] _____
- [ ] _____
- [ ] _____

Day 2
- [ ] _____
- [ ] _____
- [ ] _____
- [ ] _____
- [ ] _____

Day 3
- [ ] _____
- [ ] _____
- [ ] _____
- [ ] _____
- [ ] _____

Day 4
- [ ] _____
- [ ] _____
- [ ] _____
- [ ] _____
- [ ] _____

Day 5
- [ ] _____
- [ ] _____
- [ ] _____
- [ ] _____
- [ ] _____

Day 6
- [ ] _____
- [ ] _____
- [ ] _____
- [ ] _____
- [ ] _____

Day 7
- [ ] _____
- [ ] _____
- [ ] _____
- [ ] _____
- [ ] _____

Notes
- [ ] _____
- [ ] _____
- [ ] _____
- [ ] _____
- [ ] _____

The First Trimester (Week 8)

Weekly Plan Starting _____

Day 1
- ☐ _____
- ☐ _____
- ☐ _____
- ☐ _____
- ☐

Day 2
- ☐ _____
- ☐ _____
- ☐ _____
- ☐ _____
- ☐

Day 3
- ☐ _____
- ☐ _____
- ☐ _____
- ☐ _____
- ☐

Day 4
- ☐ _____
- ☐ _____
- ☐ _____
- ☐ _____
- ☐

Day 5
- ☐ _____
- ☐ _____
- ☐ _____
- ☐ _____
- ☐

Day 6
- ☐ _____
- ☐ _____
- ☐ _____
- ☐ _____
- ☐

Day 7
- ☐ _____
- ☐ _____
- ☐ _____
- ☐ _____
- ☐

Notes
- ☐ _____
- ☐ _____
- ☐ _____
- ☐ _____
- ☐ _____

The First Trimester (Week 9)

Weekly Plan Starting _____

Day 1
- ☐ _____
- ☐ _____
- ☐ _____
- ☐ _____
- ☐ _____

Day 2
- ☐ _____
- ☐ _____
- ☐ _____
- ☐ _____
- ☐ _____

Day 3
- ☐ _____
- ☐ _____
- ☐ _____
- ☐ _____
- ☐ _____

Day 4
- ☐ _____
- ☐ _____
- ☐ _____
- ☐ _____
- ☐ _____

Day 5
- ☐ _____
- ☐ _____
- ☐ _____
- ☐ _____
- ☐ _____

Day 6
- ☐ _____
- ☐ _____
- ☐ _____
- ☐ _____
- ☐ _____

Day 7
- ☐ _____
- ☐ _____
- ☐ _____
- ☐ _____
- ☐ _____

Notes
- ☐ _____
- ☐ _____
- ☐ _____
- ☐ _____
- ☐ _____

The First Trimester (Week 10)

Weekly Plan Starting _____

Day 1
- [ ] _____
- [ ] _____
- [ ] _____
- [ ] _____
- [ ] _____

Day 2
- [ ] _____
- [ ] _____
- [ ] _____
- [ ] _____
- [ ] _____

Day 3
- [ ] _____
- [ ] _____
- [ ] _____
- [ ] _____
- [ ] _____

Day 4
- [ ] _____
- [ ] _____
- [ ] _____
- [ ] _____
- [ ] _____

Day 5
- [ ] _____
- [ ] _____
- [ ] _____
- [ ] _____
- [ ] _____

Day 6
- [ ] _____
- [ ] _____
- [ ] _____
- [ ] _____

Day 7
- [ ] _____
- [ ] _____
- [ ] _____
- [ ] _____
- [ ] _____

Notes
- [ ] _____
- [ ] _____
- [ ] _____
- [ ] _____
- [ ] _____

The First Trimester (Week 11)

Weekly Plan Starting _____

Day 1
- ☐ _____
- ☐ _____
- ☐ _____
- ☐ _____
- ☐ _____

Day 2
- ☐ _____
- ☐ _____
- ☐ _____
- ☐ _____
- ☐ _____

Day 3
- ☐ _____
- ☐ _____
- ☐ _____
- ☐ _____
- ☐ _____

Day 4
- ☐ _____
- ☐ _____
- ☐ _____
- ☐ _____
- ☐ _____

Day 5
- ☐ _____
- ☐ _____
- ☐ _____
- ☐ _____
- ☐ _____

Day 6
- ☐ _____
- ☐ _____
- ☐ _____
- ☐ _____
- ☐ _____

Day 7
- ☐ _____
- ☐ _____
- ☐ _____
- ☐ _____
- ☐ _____

Notes
- ☐ _____
- ☐ _____
- ☐ _____
- ☐ _____
- ☐ _____

The First Trimester (Week 12)

Weekly Plan Starting _____

Day 1
- ☐ _____
- ☐ _____
- ☐ _____
- ☐ _____
- ☐ _____

Day 2
- ☐ _____
- ☐ _____
- ☐ _____
- ☐ _____
- ☐ _____

Day 3
- ☐ _____
- ☐ _____
- ☐ _____
- ☐ _____
- ☐ _____

Day 4
- ☐ _____
- ☐ _____
- ☐ _____
- ☐ _____
- ☐ _____

Day 5
- ☐ _____
- ☐ _____
- ☐ _____
- ☐ _____
- ☐ _____

Day 6
- ☐ _____
- ☐ _____
- ☐ _____
- ☐ _____

Day 7
- ☐ _____
- ☐ _____
- ☐ _____
- ☐ _____
- ☐ _____

Notes
- ☐ _____
- ☐ _____
- ☐ _____
- ☐ _____
- ☐ _____

The Second Trimester (Week 13 to 26)

> Daddy & Mommy to Note:
> Some mama will experience morning sickness in the 1st Trimester and in the 2nd Trimester, they began to feel more energetic. This is the easiest 3-months of pregnancy for most women. Between 18 th and 22nd weeks, you may learn the sex of your baby through ultrasound.
>
> Yoga pranayama practices like Ujjayi Pranayama (Victorious Breath) & Nadi Shodhana Pranayama (Alternate-Nostril breathing) can be done.
> But please seek professional advice from instructor who teaches prenatal yoga

Some yoga poses

Utthita Trikonasana
-Extended Triangle Pose

Utkatasana
- Chair Pose

Vrksasana - Tree Pose

Virabhadrasana III
- Warrior III Pose

The Second Trimester (Week 13)

Weekly Plan Starting _____

Day 1
- ☐ _____
- ☐ _____
- ☐ _____
- ☐ _____
- ☐ _____

Day 2
- ☐ _____
- ☐ _____
- ☐ _____
- ☐ _____
- ☐ _____

Day 3
- ☐ _____
- ☐ _____
- ☐ _____
- ☐ _____
- ☐ _____

Day 4
- ☐ _____
- ☐ _____
- ☐ _____
- ☐ _____
- ☐ _____

Day 5
- ☐ _____
- ☐ _____
- ☐ _____
- ☐ _____
- ☐ _____

Day 6
- ☐ _____
- ☐ _____
- ☐ _____
- ☐ _____
- ☐ _____

Day 7
- ☐ _____
- ☐ _____
- ☐ _____
- ☐ _____
- ☐ _____

Notes
- ☐ _____
- ☐ _____
- ☐ _____
- ☐ _____

The Second Trimester (Week 14)

Weekly Plan Starting _____

Day 1
- ☐ _____
- ☐ _____
- ☐ _____
- ☐ _____
- ☐ _____

Day 2
- ☐ _____
- ☐ _____
- ☐ _____
- ☐ _____
- ☐ _____

Day 3
- ☐ _____
- ☐ _____
- ☐ _____
- ☐ _____
- ☐ _____

Day 4
- ☐ _____
- ☐ _____
- ☐ _____
- ☐ _____
- ☐ _____

Day 5
- ☐ _____
- ☐ _____
- ☐ _____
- ☐ _____
- ☐ _____

Day 6
- ☐ _____
- ☐ _____
- ☐ _____
- ☐ _____
- ☐ _____

Day 7
- ☐ _____
- ☐ _____
- ☐ _____
- ☐ _____
- ☐ _____

Notes
- ☐ _____
- ☐ _____
- ☐ _____
- ☐ _____
- ☐ _____

The Second Trimester (Week 15)

Weekly Plan Starting _____

Day 1
- ☐ _____
- ☐ _____
- ☐ _____
- ☐ _____
- ☐ _____

Day 2
- ☐ _____
- ☐ _____
- ☐ _____
- ☐ _____
- ☐ _____

Day 3
- ☐ _____
- ☐ _____
- ☐ _____
- ☐ _____
- ☐ _____

Day 4
- ☐ _____
- ☐ _____
- ☐ _____
- ☐ _____
- ☐ _____

Day 5
- ☐ _____
- ☐ _____
- ☐ _____
- ☐ _____
- ☐ _____

Day 6
- ☐ _____
- ☐ _____
- ☐ _____
- ☐ _____
- ☐ _____

Day 7
- ☐ _____
- ☐ _____
- ☐ _____
- ☐ _____
- ☐ _____

Notes
- ☐ _____
- ☐ _____
- ☐ _____
- ☐ _____
- ☐ _____

The Second Trimester (Week 16)

Weekly Plan Starting _____

Day 1
- ☐ _____
- ☐ _____
- ☐ _____
- ☐ _____
- ☐

Day 2
- ☐ _____
- ☐ _____
- ☐ _____
- ☐ _____
- ☐ _____

Day 3
- ☐ _____
- ☐ _____
- ☐ _____
- ☐ _____
- ☐

Day 4
- ☐ _____
- ☐ _____
- ☐ _____
- ☐ _____
- ☐

Day 5
- ☐ _____
- ☐ _____
- ☐ _____
- ☐ _____
- ☐

Day 6
- ☐ _____
- ☐ _____
- ☐ _____
- ☐ _____

Day 7
- ☐ _____
- ☐ _____
- ☐ _____
- ☐ _____
- ☐

Notes
- ☐ _____
- ☐ _____
- ☐ _____
- ☐ _____
- ☐

The Second Trimester (Week 17)

Weekly Plan Starting _____

Day 1
- ☐ _____
- ☐ _____
- ☐ _____
- ☐ _____
- ☐ _____

Day 2
- ☐ _____
- ☐ _____
- ☐ _____
- ☐ _____
- ☐ _____

Day 3
- ☐ _____
- ☐ _____
- ☐ _____
- ☐ _____
- ☐ _____

Day 4
- ☐ _____
- ☐ _____
- ☐ _____
- ☐ _____
- ☐ _____

Day 5
- ☐ _____
- ☐ _____
- ☐ _____
- ☐ _____
- ☐ _____

Day 6
- ☐ _____
- ☐ _____
- ☐ _____
- ☐ _____
- ☐ _____

Day 7
- ☐ _____
- ☐ _____
- ☐ _____
- ☐ _____
- ☐ _____

Notes
- ☐ _____
- ☐ _____
- ☐ _____
- ☐ _____
- ☐ _____

The Second Trimester (Week 18)

Weekly Plan Starting _____

Day 1

- ☐ _____
- ☐ _____
- ☐ _____
- ☐ _____
- ☐ _____

Day 2

- ☐ _____
- ☐ _____
- ☐ _____
- ☐ _____
- ☐ _____

Day 3

- ☐ _____
- ☐ _____
- ☐ _____
- ☐ _____
- ☐ _____

Day 4

- ☐ _____
- ☐ _____
- ☐ _____
- ☐ _____
- ☐ _____

Day 5

- ☐ _____
- ☐ _____
- ☐ _____
- ☐ _____
- ☐ _____

Day 6

- ☐ _____
- ☐ _____
- ☐ _____
- ☐ _____
- ☐ _____

Day 7

- ☐ _____
- ☐ _____
- ☐ _____
- ☐ _____
- ☐ _____

Notes

- ☐ _____
- ☐ _____
- ☐ _____
- ☐ _____
- ☐ _____

The Second Trimester (Week 19)

Weekly Plan Starting _____

Day 1
- [ ] _____
- [ ] _____
- [ ] _____
- [ ] _____
- [ ] _____

Day 2
- [ ] _____
- [ ] _____
- [ ] _____
- [ ] _____
- [ ] _____

Day 3
- [ ] _____
- [ ] _____
- [ ] _____
- [ ] _____
- [ ] _____

Day 4
- [ ] _____
- [ ] _____
- [ ] _____
- [ ] _____
- [ ] _____

Day 5
- [ ] _____
- [ ] _____
- [ ] _____
- [ ] _____
- [ ] _____

Day 6
- [ ] _____
- [ ] _____
- [ ] _____
- [ ] _____
- [ ] _____

Day 7
- [ ] _____
- [ ] _____
- [ ] _____
- [ ] _____
- [ ] _____

Notes
- [ ] _____
- [ ] _____
- [ ] _____
- [ ] _____
- [ ] _____

The Second Trimester (Week 20)

Weekly Plan Starting _____

Day 1

- ❏ _____
- ❏ _____
- ❏ _____
- ❏ _____
- ❏ _____

Day 2

- ❏ _____
- ❏ _____
- ❏ _____
- ❏ _____
- ❏ _____

Day 3

- ❏ _____
- ❏ _____
- ❏ _____
- ❏ _____
- ❏ _____

Day 4

- ❏ _____
- ❏ _____
- ❏ _____
- ❏ _____
- ❏ _____

Day 5

- ❏ _____
- ❏ _____
- ❏ _____
- ❏ _____
- ❏ _____

Day 6

- ❏ _____
- ❏ _____
- ❏ _____
- ❏ _____
- ❏ _____

Day 7

- ❏ _____
- ❏ _____
- ❏ _____
- ❏ _____
- ❏ _____

Notes

- ❏ _____
- ❏ _____
- ❏ _____
- ❏ _____
- ❏ _____

The Second Trimester (Week 21)

Weekly Plan Starting _____

Day 1
- ☐ _____
- ☐ _____
- ☐ _____
- ☐ _____
- ☐ _____

Day 2
- ☐ _____
- ☐ _____
- ☐ _____
- ☐ _____
- ☐ _____

Day 3
- ☐ _____
- ☐ _____
- ☐ _____
- ☐ _____
- ☐ _____

Day 4
- ☐ _____
- ☐ _____
- ☐ _____
- ☐ _____
- ☐ _____

Day 5
- ☐ _____
- ☐ _____
- ☐ _____
- ☐ _____
- ☐ _____

Day 6
- ☐ _____
- ☐ _____
- ☐ _____
- ☐ _____
- ☐ _____

Day 7
- ☐ _____
- ☐ _____
- ☐ _____
- ☐ _____
- ☐ _____

Notes
- ☐ _____
- ☐ _____
- ☐ _____
- ☐ _____
- ☐ _____

The Second Trimester (Week 22)

Weekly Plan Starting _____

Day 1
- [ ] _____
- [ ] _____
- [ ] _____
- [ ] _____
- [ ] _____

Day 2
- [ ] _____
- [ ] _____
- [ ] _____
- [ ] _____
- [ ] _____

Day 3
- [ ] _____
- [ ] _____
- [ ] _____
- [ ] _____
- [ ] _____

Day 4
- [ ] _____
- [ ] _____
- [ ] _____
- [ ] _____
- [ ] _____

Day 5
- [ ] _____
- [ ] _____
- [ ] _____
- [ ] _____
- [ ] _____

Day 6
- [ ] _____
- [ ] _____
- [ ] _____
- [ ] _____
- [ ] _____

Day 7
- [ ] _____
- [ ] _____
- [ ] _____
- [ ] _____
- [ ] _____

Notes
- [ ] _____
- [ ] _____
- [ ] _____
- [ ] _____
- [ ] _____

The Second Trimester (Week 23)

Weekly Plan Starting _____

Day 1
- ☐ _____
- ☐ _____
- ☐ _____
- ☐ _____
- ☐ _____

Day 2
- ☐ _____
- ☐ _____
- ☐ _____
- ☐ _____
- ☐ _____

Day 3
- ☐ _____
- ☐ _____
- ☐ _____
- ☐ _____
- ☐ _____

Day 4
- ☐ _____
- ☐ _____
- ☐ _____
- ☐ _____
- ☐ _____

Day 5
- ☐ _____
- ☐ _____
- ☐ _____
- ☐ _____
- ☐ _____

Day 6
- ☐ _____
- ☐ _____
- ☐ _____
- ☐ _____
- ☐ _____

Day 7
- ☐ _____
- ☐ _____
- ☐ _____
- ☐ _____
- ☐ _____

Notes
- ☐ _____
- ☐ _____
- ☐ _____
- ☐ _____
- ☐ _____

The Second Trimester (Week 24)

Weekly Plan Starting _____

Day 1

- [ ] _____
- [ ] _____
- [ ] _____
- [ ] _____
- [ ]

Day 2

- [ ] _____
- [ ] _____
- [ ] _____
- [ ] _____
- [ ] _____

Day 3

- [ ] _____
- [ ] _____
- [ ] _____
- [ ] _____
- [ ] _____

Day 4

- [ ] _____
- [ ] _____
- [ ] _____
- [ ] _____
- [ ]

Day 5

- [ ] _____
- [ ] _____
- [ ] _____
- [ ] _____
- [ ]

Day 6

- [ ] _____
- [ ] _____
- [ ] _____
- [ ] _____
- [ ] _____

Day 7

- [ ] _____
- [ ] _____
- [ ] _____
- [ ] _____
- [ ] _____

Notes

- [ ] _____
- [ ] _____
- [ ] _____
- [ ] _____
- [ ] _____

The Second Trimester (Week 25)

Weekly Plan Starting _____

Day 1
- [ ] _____
- [ ] _____
- [ ] _____
- [ ] _____
- [ ] _____

Day 2
- [ ] _____
- [ ] _____
- [ ] _____
- [ ] _____
- [ ] _____

Day 3
- [ ] _____
- [ ] _____
- [ ] _____
- [ ] _____
- [ ] _____

Day 4
- [ ] _____
- [ ] _____
- [ ] _____
- [ ] _____
- [ ] _____

Day 5
- [ ] _____
- [ ] _____
- [ ] _____
- [ ] _____
- [ ] _____

Day 6
- [ ] _____
- [ ] _____
- [ ] _____
- [ ] _____
- [ ] _____

Day 7
- [ ] _____
- [ ] _____
- [ ] _____
- [ ] _____
- [ ] _____

Notes
- [ ] _____
- [ ] _____
- [ ] _____
- [ ] _____
- [ ] _____

The Second Trimester (Week 26)

Weekly Plan Starting _____

Day 1
- ☐ _____
- ☐ _____
- ☐ _____
- ☐ _____
- ☐ _____

Day 2
- ☐ _____
- ☐ _____
- ☐ _____
- ☐ _____
- ☐ _____

Day 3
- ☐ _____
- ☐ _____
- ☐ _____
- ☐ _____
- ☐ _____

Day 4
- ☐ _____
- ☐ _____
- ☐ _____
- ☐ _____
- ☐ _____

Day 5
- ☐ _____
- ☐ _____
- ☐ _____
- ☐ _____
- ☐ _____

Day 6
- ☐ _____
- ☐ _____
- ☐ _____
- ☐ _____
- ☐ _____

Day 7
- ☐ _____
- ☐ _____
- ☐ _____
- ☐ _____
- ☐ _____

Notes
- ☐ _____
- ☐ _____
- ☐ _____
- ☐ _____
- ☐ _____

Last Trimester (Week 27 to 40)

> Daddy & Mommy to Note:
> Hurray! In 3 more months, your little Baby will be born. However, this will be the period where wife will feel extra weight adding pressure on her back making it achy and sore.
> Daddy's gentle massage and comfort message is very important.
> Have you done all the necessary for the new arrival? Remember to get ready the bag to hospital.
>
> Some yoga poses can be practice to ease any physical discomfort and preparing for labor.
> To seek advice from instructor who teaches prenatal yoga.

Some yoga poses

Utthita Trikonasana
-Extended Triangle Pose

Virabhadrasana I
-Warrior I Pose

Vrksasana - Tree Pose

Baddha Konasana
- Bound Angle Pose

Last Trimester (Week 27)

Weekly Plan Starting _____

Day 1

- ☐ _____
- ☐ _____
- ☐ _____
- ☐ _____
- ☐ _____

Day 2

- ☐ _____
- ☐ _____
- ☐ _____
- ☐ _____
- ☐ _____

Day 3

- ☐ _____
- ☐ _____
- ☐ _____
- ☐ _____
- ☐ _____

Day 4

- ☐ _____
- ☐ _____
- ☐ _____
- ☐ _____
- ☐ _____

Day 5

- ☐ _____
- ☐ _____
- ☐ _____
- ☐ _____
- ☐ _____

Day 6

- ☐ _____
- ☐ _____
- ☐ _____
- ☐ _____
- ☐ _____

Day 7

- ☐ _____
- ☐ _____
- ☐ _____
- ☐ _____
- ☐ _____

Notes

- ☐ _____
- ☐ _____
- ☐ _____
- ☐ _____
- ☐ _____

Last Trimester (Week 28)

Weekly Plan Starting _____

Day 1

- ☐ _____
- ☐ _____
- ☐ _____
- ☐ _____
- ☐ _____

Day 2

- ☐ _____
- ☐ _____
- ☐ _____
- ☐ _____
- ☐ _____

Day 3

- ☐ _____
- ☐ _____
- ☐ _____
- ☐ _____
- ☐ _____

Day 4

- ☐ _____
- ☐ _____
- ☐ _____
- ☐ _____
- ☐ _____

Day 5

- ☐ _____
- ☐ _____
- ☐ _____
- ☐ _____
- ☐ _____

Day 6

- ☐ _____
- ☐ _____
- ☐ _____
- ☐ _____
- ☐ _____

Day 7

- ☐ _____
- ☐ _____
- ☐ _____
- ☐ _____
- ☐ _____

Notes

- ☐ _____
- ☐ _____
- ☐ _____
- ☐ _____
- ☐ _____

Last Trimester (Week 29)

Weekly Plan Starting _____

Day 1
- [ ] _____
- [ ] _____
- [ ] _____
- [ ] _____
- [ ] _____

Day 2
- [ ] _____
- [ ] _____
- [ ] _____
- [ ] _____
- [ ] _____

Day 3
- [ ] _____
- [ ] _____
- [ ] _____
- [ ] _____
- [ ] _____

Day 4
- [ ] _____
- [ ] _____
- [ ] _____
- [ ] _____
- [ ] _____

Day 5
- [ ] _____
- [ ] _____
- [ ] _____
- [ ] _____
- [ ] _____

Day 6
- [ ] _____
- [ ] _____
- [ ] _____
- [ ] _____
- [ ] _____

Day 7
- [ ] _____
- [ ] _____
- [ ] _____
- [ ] _____
- [ ] _____

Notes
- [ ] _____
- [ ] _____
- [ ] _____
- [ ] _____
- [ ] _____

Last Trimester (Week 30)

Weekly Plan Starting _____

Day 1
- ☐ _____
- ☐ _____
- ☐ _____
- ☐ _____
- ☐ _____

Day 2
- ☐ _____
- ☐ _____
- ☐ _____
- ☐ _____
- ☐ _____

Day 3
- ☐ _____
- ☐ _____
- ☐ _____
- ☐ _____
- ☐ _____

Day 4
- ☐ _____
- ☐ _____
- ☐ _____
- ☐ _____
- ☐ _____

Day 5
- ☐ _____
- ☐ _____
- ☐ _____
- ☐ _____
- ☐ _____

Day 6
- ☐ _____
- ☐ _____
- ☐ _____
- ☐ _____
- ☐ _____

Day 7
- ☐ _____
- ☐ _____
- ☐ _____
- ☐ _____
- ☐ _____

Notes
- ☐ _____
- ☐ _____
- ☐ _____
- ☐ _____
- ☐ _____

Last Trimester (Week 31)

Weekly Plan Starting _____

Day 1

- [ ] _____
- [ ] _____
- [ ] _____
- [ ] _____
- [ ] _____

Day 2

- [ ] _____
- [ ] _____
- [ ] _____
- [ ] _____
- [ ] _____

Day 3

- [ ] _____
- [ ] _____
- [ ] _____
- [ ] _____
- [ ] _____

Day 4

- [ ] _____
- [ ] _____
- [ ] _____
- [ ] _____
- [ ] _____

Day 5

- [ ] _____
- [ ] _____
- [ ] _____
- [ ] _____
- [ ] _____

Day 6

- [ ] _____
- [ ] _____
- [ ] _____
- [ ] _____
- [ ] _____

Day 7

- [ ] _____
- [ ] _____
- [ ] _____
- [ ] _____
- [ ] _____

Notes

- [ ] _____
- [ ] _____
- [ ] _____
- [ ] _____
- [ ] _____

Last Trimester (Week 32)

Weekly Plan Starting _____

Day 1
- ☐ _____
- ☐ _____
- ☐ _____
- ☐ _____
- ☐ _____

Day 2
- ☐ _____
- ☐ _____
- ☐ _____
- ☐ _____
- ☐ _____

Day 3
- ☐ _____
- ☐ _____
- ☐ _____
- ☐ _____
- ☐ _____

Day 4
- ☐ _____
- ☐ _____
- ☐ _____
- ☐ _____
- ☐ _____

Day 5
- ☐ _____
- ☐ _____
- ☐ _____
- ☐ _____
- ☐ _____

Day 6
- ☐ _____
- ☐ _____
- ☐ _____
- ☐ _____
- ☐ _____

Day 7
- ☐ _____
- ☐ _____
- ☐ _____
- ☐ _____
- ☐ _____

Notes
- ☐ _____
- ☐ _____
- ☐ _____
- ☐ _____
- ☐ _____

Last Trimester (Week 33)

Weekly Plan Starting _____

Day 1
- ☐ _____
- ☐ _____
- ☐ _____
- ☐ _____
- ☐ _____

Day 2
- ☐ _____
- ☐ _____
- ☐ _____
- ☐ _____
- ☐ _____

Day 3
- ☐ _____
- ☐ _____
- ☐ _____
- ☐ _____
- ☐ _____

Day 4
- ☐ _____
- ☐ _____
- ☐ _____
- ☐ _____
- ☐ _____

Day 5
- ☐ _____
- ☐ _____
- ☐ _____
- ☐ _____
- ☐ _____

Day 6
- ☐ _____
- ☐ _____
- ☐ _____
- ☐ _____
- ☐ _____

Day 7
- ☐ _____
- ☐ _____
- ☐ _____
- ☐ _____
- ☐ _____

Notes
- ☐ _____
- ☐ _____
- ☐ _____
- ☐ _____
- ☐ _____

Last Trimester (Week 34)

Weekly Plan Starting _____

Day 1

- ❑ _____
- ❑ _____
- ❑ _____
- ❑ _____
- ❑ _____

Day 2

- ❑ _____
- ❑ _____
- ❑ _____
- ❑ _____
- ❑ _____

Day 3

- ❑ _____
- ❑ _____
- ❑ _____
- ❑ _____
- ❑ _____

Day 4

- ❑ _____
- ❑ _____
- ❑ _____
- ❑ _____
- ❑ _____

Day 5

- ❑ _____
- ❑ _____
- ❑ _____
- ❑ _____
- ❑ _____

Day 6

- ❑ _____
- ❑ _____
- ❑ _____
- ❑ _____
- ❑ _____

Day 7

- ❑ _____
- ❑ _____
- ❑ _____
- ❑ _____
- ❑ _____

Notes

- ❑ _____
- ❑ _____
- ❑ _____
- ❑ _____
- ❑ _____

Last Trimester (Week 35)

Weekly Plan Starting _____

Day 1

- [ ] _____
- [ ] _____
- [ ] _____
- [ ] _____
- [ ] _____

Day 2

- [ ] _____
- [ ] _____
- [ ] _____
- [ ] _____
- [ ] _____

Day 3

- [ ] _____
- [ ] _____
- [ ] _____
- [ ] _____
- [ ] _____

Day 4

- [ ] _____
- [ ] _____
- [ ] _____
- [ ] _____
- [ ] _____

Day 5

- [ ] _____
- [ ] _____
- [ ] _____
- [ ] _____
- [ ] _____

Day 6

- [ ] _____
- [ ] _____
- [ ] _____
- [ ] _____
- [ ] _____

Day 7

- [ ] _____
- [ ] _____
- [ ] _____
- [ ] _____
- [ ] _____

Notes

- [ ] _____
- [ ] _____
- [ ] _____
- [ ] _____
- [ ] _____

Last Trimester (Week 36)

Weekly Plan Starting _____

Day 1
- ❑ _____
- ❑ _____
- ❑ _____
- ❑ _____
- ❑ _____

Day 2
- ❑ _____
- ❑ _____
- ❑ _____
- ❑ _____
- ❑ _____

Day 3
- ❑ _____
- ❑ _____
- ❑ _____
- ❑ _____
- ❑ _____

Day 4
- ❑ _____
- ❑ _____
- ❑ _____
- ❑ _____
- ❑ _____

Day 5
- ❑ _____
- ❑ _____
- ❑ _____
- ❑ _____
- ❑ _____

Day 6
- ❑ _____
- ❑ _____
- ❑ _____
- ❑ _____
- ❑ _____

Day 7
- ❑ _____
- ❑ _____
- ❑ _____
- ❑ _____
- ❑ _____

Notes
- ❑ _____
- ❑ _____
- ❑ _____
- ❑ _____
- ❑ _____

Last Trimester (Week 37)

Weekly Plan Starting _____

Day 1
- ☐ _____
- ☐ _____
- ☐ _____
- ☐ _____
- ☐ _____

Day 2
- ☐ _____
- ☐ _____
- ☐ _____
- ☐ _____
- ☐ _____

Day 3
- ☐ _____
- ☐ _____
- ☐ _____
- ☐ _____
- ☐ _____

Day 4
- ☐ _____
- ☐ _____
- ☐ _____
- ☐ _____
- ☐ _____

Day 5
- ☐ _____
- ☐ _____
- ☐ _____
- ☐ _____
- ☐ _____

Day 6
- ☐ _____
- ☐ _____
- ☐ _____
- ☐ _____
- ☐ _____

Day 7
- ☐ _____
- ☐ _____
- ☐ _____
- ☐ _____
- ☐ _____

Notes
- ☐ _____
- ☐ _____
- ☐ _____
- ☐ _____
- ☐ _____

Last Trimester (Week 38)

Weekly Plan Starting _____

Day 1
- [ ] _____
- [ ] _____
- [ ] _____
- [ ] _____
- [ ] _____

Day 2
- [ ] _____
- [ ] _____
- [ ] _____
- [ ] _____
- [ ] _____

Day 3
- [ ] _____
- [ ] _____
- [ ] _____
- [ ] _____
- [ ] _____

Day 4
- [ ] _____
- [ ] _____
- [ ] _____
- [ ] _____
- [ ] _____

Day 5
- [ ] _____
- [ ] _____
- [ ] _____
- [ ] _____
- [ ] _____

Day 6
- [ ] _____
- [ ] _____
- [ ] _____
- [ ] _____
- [ ] _____

Day 7
- [ ] _____
- [ ] _____
- [ ] _____
- [ ] _____
- [ ] _____

Notes
- [ ] _____
- [ ] _____
- [ ] _____
- [ ] _____
- [ ] _____

Last Trimester (Week 39)

Weekly Plan Starting _____

Day 1

- ☐ _____
- ☐ _____
- ☐ _____
- ☐ _____
- ☐ _____

Day 2

- ☐ _____
- ☐ _____
- ☐ _____
- ☐ _____
- ☐ _____

Day 3

- ☐ _____
- ☐ _____
- ☐ _____
- ☐ _____
- ☐ _____

Day 4

- ☐ _____
- ☐ _____
- ☐ _____
- ☐ _____
- ☐ _____

Day 5

- ☐ _____
- ☐ _____
- ☐ _____
- ☐ _____
- ☐ _____

Day 6

- ☐ _____
- ☐ _____
- ☐ _____
- ☐ _____
- ☐ _____

Day 7

- ☐ _____
- ☐ _____
- ☐ _____
- ☐ _____
- ☐ _____

Notes

- ☐ _____
- ☐ _____
- ☐ _____
- ☐ _____
- ☐ _____

Last Trimester (Week 40)

Weekly Plan Starting _____

Day 1
- [ ] _____
- [ ] _____
- [ ] _____
- [ ] _____
- [ ] _____

Day 2
- [ ] _____
- [ ] _____
- [ ] _____
- [ ] _____
- [ ] _____

Day 3
- [ ] _____
- [ ] _____
- [ ] _____
- [ ] _____
- [ ] _____

Day 4
- [ ] _____
- [ ] _____
- [ ] _____
- [ ] _____
- [ ] _____

Day 5
- [ ] _____
- [ ] _____
- [ ] _____
- [ ] _____
- [ ] _____

Day 6
- [ ] _____
- [ ] _____
- [ ] _____
- [ ] _____
- [ ] _____

Day 7
- [ ] _____
- [ ] _____
- [ ] _____
- [ ] _____
- [ ] _____

Notes
- [ ] _____
- [ ] _____
- [ ] _____
- [ ] _____
- [ ] _____

> My Little Darling,
>
> Our precious memory filling up the whole Book from the day you are with us.

Our 1st Family Photo

Add Photo Here

Your First Cry ...

Your First Month ...

Date ___ / ___ / ___

Thanks for being with us...

Date ___ / ___ / ___

I am so Blessed ...

Date ____ / ____ / ____

You sparkle up my life ...

Date ___/___/___

You are my everything ... Date ___ / ___ / ___

You are such a sweetie...

You are my sweetheart...   Date ___ / ___ / ___

Thanks for being with us... Date ___/___/___

My Darling,
I love you !

Your First Drawing

Add Photo Here

My Sweetheart,

Remember, Mommy & Daddy will always be there for you!

**Thank you so much for your support &
hope you have enjoyed every moment!**

Please help to leave a good review in Amazon.com

Made in the USA
Middletown, DE
31 March 2021